SUPER SNAKES

CORAL SNAKE

Murray "Oak" Tapeta

NorwoodHouse Press

Cataloging-in-Publication Data

Names: Tapeta, Murray.
Title: Coral snake / Murray Tapeta.
Description: Buffalo, NY : Norwood House Press, 2026. | Series: Super snakes | Includes glossary and index.
Identifiers: ISBN 9781978575103 (pbk.) | ISBN 9781978575110 (library bound) | ISBN 9781978575127 (ebook)
Subjects: LCSH: Coral snakes--Juvenile literature.
Classification: LCC QL666.O64 T374 2026 | DDC 597.96'44--dc23

Published in 2026 by
Norwood House Press
2544 Clinton Street
Buffalo, NY 14224

Designer: Rhea Magaro
Editor: Kim Thompson

Photo credits: Cover, p. 1, 5 Vaclav Sebek/Shutterstock.com; p. 3 Francesca Leslie/Shutterstock.com; P. 5 Jay Ondreicka/Shutterstock.com; p. 6 Mark_Kostich/Shutterstock.com; p. 7 Taufan Nurzaman Sulaeman/Shutterstock.com; pp. 8, 9 mspoli/Shutterstock.com; p. 10 Rich Carey/Shutterstock.com; p. 11 jokerbethyname/Shutterstock.com; pp. 12, 13 Chase D'animulls/Shutterstock.com; p. 15 biozeca/Shutterstock.com; p. 16 Andrew Jeffries/Shutterstock.com; p. 17 Rick Neves/Shutterstock.com; p. 18 Moment of Perception/Shutterstock.com; p. 19 Matt Jeppson/Shutterstock.com; p. 20 Arjun9810/Shutterstock.com; p. 21 Alexander Wong/Shutterstock.com;

Printed in the United States of America

CPSIA compliance information: Batch #CSNHP26: For further information contact Norwood House Press at 1-800-237-9932.

TABLE OF CONTENTS

What Is Special about Coral Snakes?

Coral snakes are small but deadly. Rings of bright color make them easy to spot. Their bite carries powerful **venom** that **paralyzes** enemies.

What Do Coral Snakes Look Like?

There are more than 80 **species** of coral snakes. Most are red, black, yellow, and white. Some are orange and gray.

Nearly all coral snakes have **markings**. Most have colored bands circling their bodies. A few have long stripes that go from head to tail.

Coral snakes are short and slender. The Sonoran coral snake grows up to 21 inches (53 centimeters) long.

It can be hard to tell a coral snake's head from its tail. When the snake is threatened, it buries its head in its **coils**. It raises its tail to trick attackers and to keep its head safe.

Where Do Coral Snakes Live?

Coral snakes live in Asia, North America, Central America, and South America. They are found in many **habitats**. Some live in water.

Coral snakes hide in animal tunnels, in hollow logs, and under rocks. This helps them avoid **predators** and maintain their body temperature.

How Do Coral Snakes Hunt?

Coral snakes hunt at night. Their **forked** tongues taste the air to help them track prey.

Coral snakes look for lizards, insects, and smaller snakes. They also hunt frogs, birds, and rodents.

A coral snake bites with short **fangs** and sharp lower teeth. It chews on the victim's body to inject venom. Its fangs are not **retractable**. After biting, the snake hangs on.

Coral snake venom paralyzes the muscles of prey animals. It makes them unable to breathe. It can take 18 hours for the victim to die.

Coral snakes attack only when bothered.

They rarely bite humans.

Coral snakes are hunted by hawks and falcons. They are also attacked by bullfrogs and larger snakes.

When a Sonoran coral snake feels threatened, it makes a popping sound. It releases a gassy smell to startle predators.

How Do Coral Snakes Reproduce?

Most female coral snakes lay eggs in a hidden place once a year. An Eastern coral snake lays up to 12 eggs.

The mother does not watch over the eggs. The eggs hatch after two months. Babies care for themselves as soon as they are born.

Glossary

coils (koilz): a series of loops, like those formed by a snake's wrapped-up body

fangs (fangz): long, pointed teeth

forked (forkd): divided into two branches or points

habitats (HAB-i-tats): places where animals usually live in the wild, such as deserts or forests

markings (MAHRK-ingz): colored lines, shapes, or patterns on the surface of something

paralyzes (PAR-uh-lye-zis): makes something powerless and unable to act or move

predators (PRED-uh-turz): animals that hunt other animals for food

retractable (ri-TRAK-tuh-buhl): able to be pulled back

species (SPEE-seez): groups of similar living things that can reproduce with each other

venom (VEN-uhm): a toxic substance that is produced by an animal to harm or kill prey and enemies

Thinking Questions

1. On what continents do coral snakes live?
2. What animals are a danger to coral snakes?
3. What do coral snakes eat?
4. Where do coral snakes hide?
5. What happens after a female coral snake lays her eggs?

Index

About the Author

Murray "Oak" Tapeta was born in a cabin without plumbing in Montana. Growing up in the great outdoors, he became a lover of nature. He earned the nickname "Oak" after climbing to the top of an oak tree at the age of three. Oak loves to read and write. He has written many books about events in history and other subjects that fascinate him. He prefers spending time in the wilderness with his dog Birchy.